Introducing The Positions

for CELLO — Volume 1   THE FOURTH POSITION

There are many students today, who, after an elementary training in cello playing, restricted entirely to the first position of their instrument, have joined the ranks of school and amateur orchestras. As the real purpose of position playing is to extend the tonal range of the cello, those students who play only in the first position, by necessity, have no alternative than to remain in elementary ensemble groups. They cannot become members of advanced school orchestras or semi-professional groups, because of their inability to play in the higher positions of their instrument. When an attempt is made to study these higher positions, they either find themselves confronted with an array of ungraded technical material, completely inadequate for their particular needs, or else find that the material to be studied in each of the several positions is not sufficient in quantity in any one book to be of real service to them.

In actuality, there are seven so called "neck" positions on the cello, the first four of which utilize the bass clef, and the last three (fifth, sixth, and seventh) the tenor clef. Beyond the seventh position there exist the "thumb" positions, which are used only in advanced cello playing. The higher positions with which the cellist first should become familiar are the second, third, and fourth, as the tonal range covered by these positions is quite adequate for playing much of the literature encountered in the orchestra of today.

As Introducing the Positions, for cello, constitutes purely an introductory course in position playing, it takes up only the second, third, and fourth positions. Of these positions, the fourth is the most important, and should be studied before the others, as it gives the students, at once, a grasp of the range of the cello most needed. Therefore, Volume One of Introducing the Positions is given over entirely to the fourth position, with shifting from the first to the fourth position, and from the fourth position back to the first position. Volume Two of Introducing the Positions takes up the second position, second-and-a-half position, third position, and third-and-a-half position, with shifting to and from these various positions.

After students have mastered the material presented in Volumes One and Two of Introducing the Positions for cello, they will have had adequate preparation for going ahead with more advanced work, such as studying the fifth, sixth, and seventh positions, as well as the various thumb positions. For this study, it is recommended that students turn to the traditional technical studies and etudes of cello literature, such as the works of Werner, Kummer, Dotzauer, Duport, Schroeder, and Davidoff.

If Introducing the Positions for cello proves itself a boon to those ambitious students in quest of material and procedures that will enable them to become better performers on their instrument, and thus become qualified for membership in advanced orchestras and ensembles, as well as more proficient in solo playing, the writer will feel gratified to know that his humble efforts have been of some educational significance.

Harvey S. Whistler, Ph. D.

RUBANK®

HAL•LEONARD®
CORPORATION
7777 W BLUEMOUND RD PO BOX 13819 MILWAUKEE, WI 53213

In memory of Leo Schulz, whose teaching methods and musical ideals were an inspiration to the author in preparing the present work.

The Fourth Position
A String

A STRING FINGERING

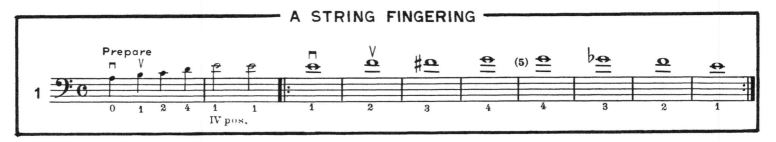

PREPARATORY STUDIES

Copyright MCMXLVII by Rubank,Inc.,Chicago,Ill.
International Copyright Secured

7

8

9

10

11

12

13

D String

D STRING FINGERING

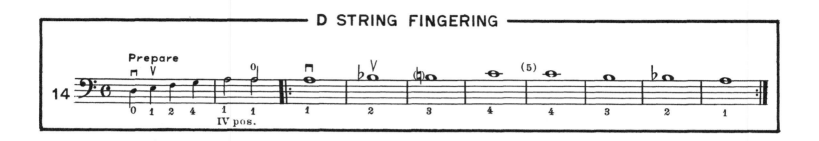

PREPARATORY STUDIES

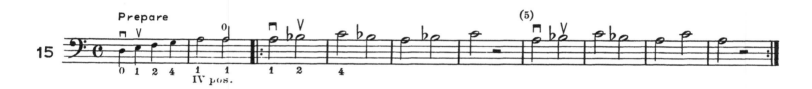

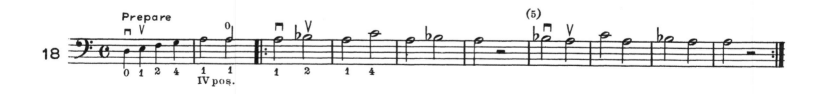

20

21

22

23

24

25

26

G String

G STRING FINGERING

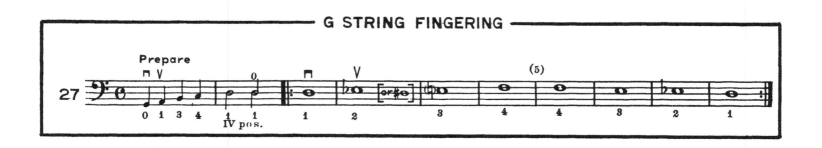

PREPARATORY STUDIES

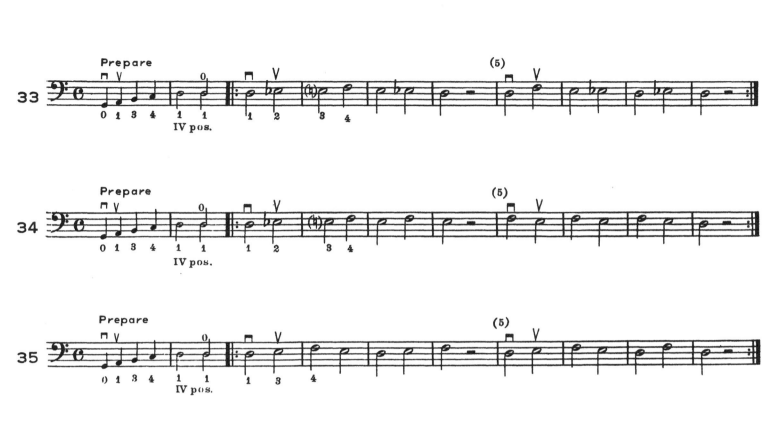

C String

C STRING FINGERING

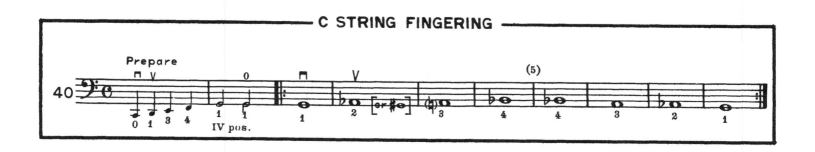

PREPARATORY STUDIES

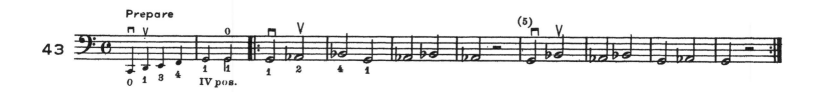

46

47

48

49

50

51

52

Technic Builders in Fourth Position

A String

Also practice technic builders (1) slurring each two tones, and (2) slurring each complete measure.

Before commencing prepare for the FOURTH POSITION by playing

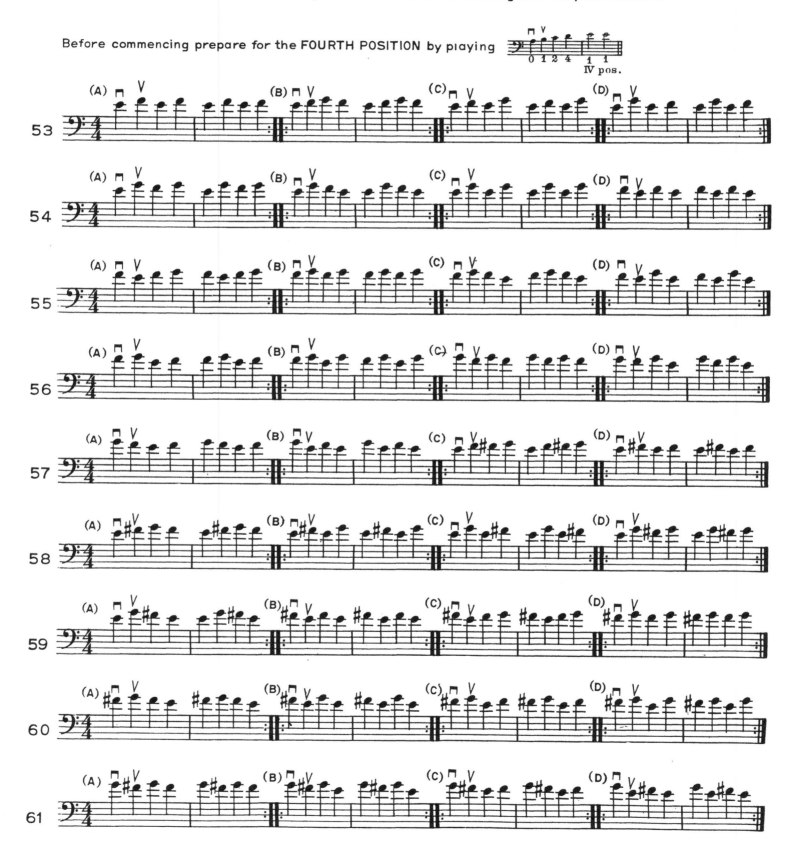

D String

Before commencing, prepare for the FOURTH POSITION by playing

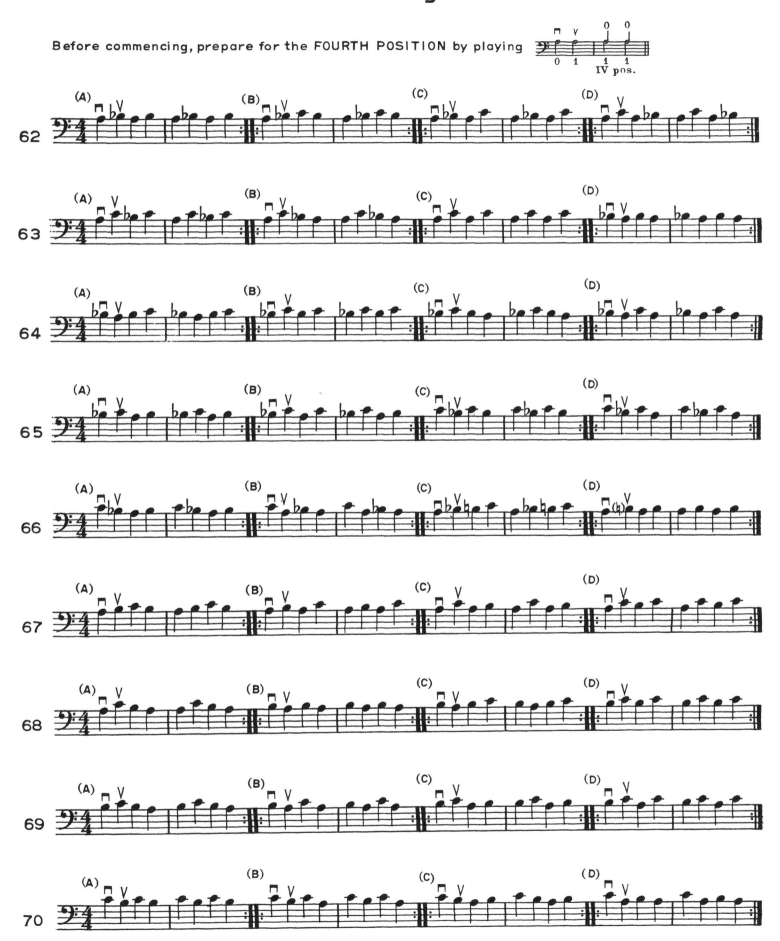

G String

Before commencing, prepare for the FOURTH POSITION by playing

71

72

73

74

75

76

77

78

79

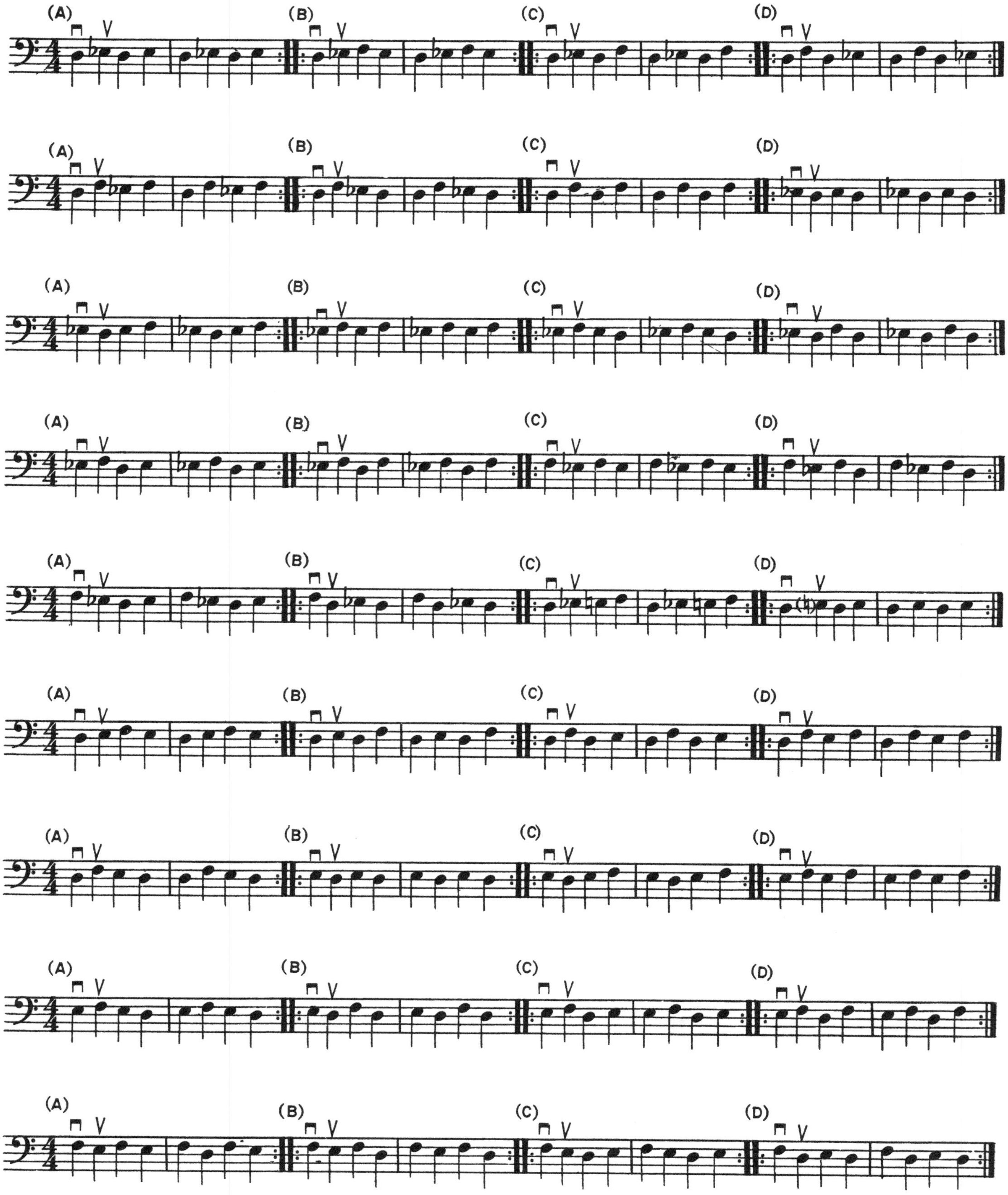

C String

Before commencing, prepare for the FOURTH POSITION by playing

Shifting from First to Fourth Position

When shifting from the first to a higher position do not take the finger up and put it down again; instead, SLIDE into the higher position.

A STRING

D STRING

G STRING

C STRING

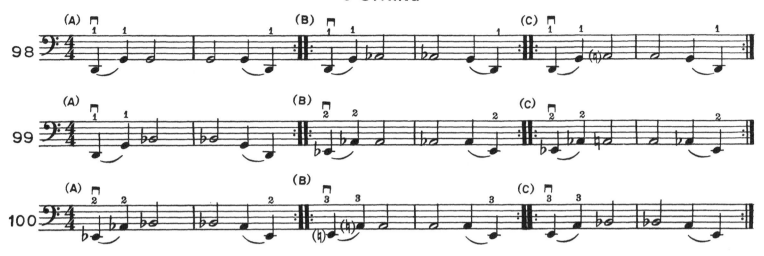

Shifting from One Finger to Another

The student should shift forward on the finger that was last down, and likewise, shift backward on the finger that was last down.

The small note in the following exercises indicates the movement of the finger in shifting, and as the student perfects his ability to shift from one note to another, the small note eventually should not be heard.

Lowered Form of Fourth Position
A String

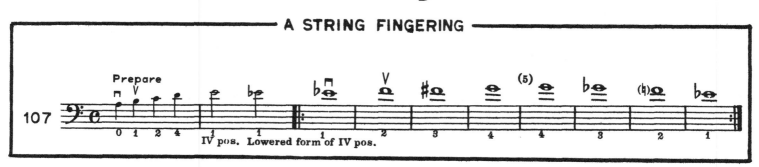

Before commencing, prepare for the LOWERED FORM OF FOURTH POSITION by playing

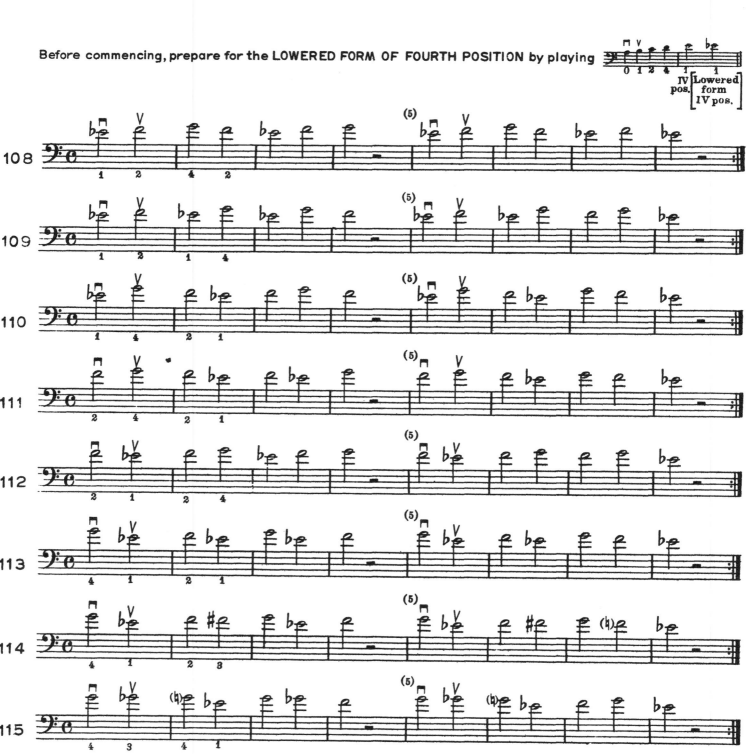

D String

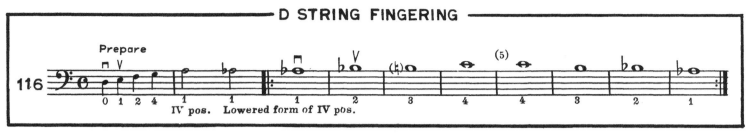

Before commencing, prepare for the LOWERED FORM OF FOURTH POSITION by playing

G String

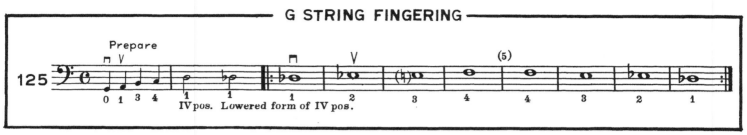

Before commencing, prepare for the **LOWERED FORM OF FOURTH POSITION** by playing

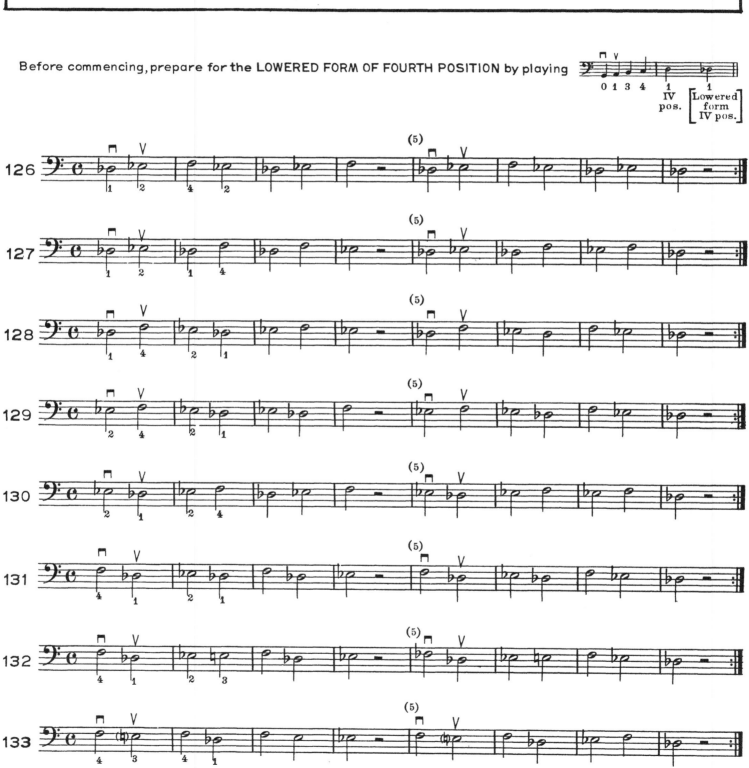

C String

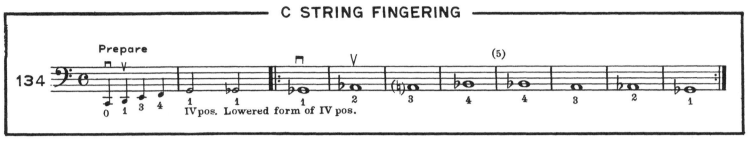

Before commencing, prepare for the LOWERED FORM OF FOURTH POSITION by playing

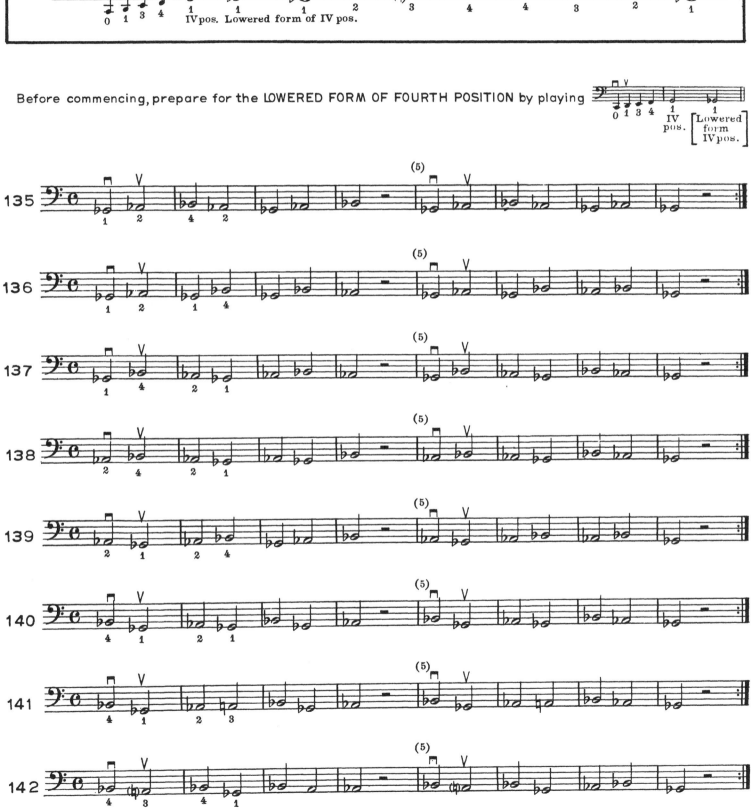

Extended Form of Fourth Position
A String

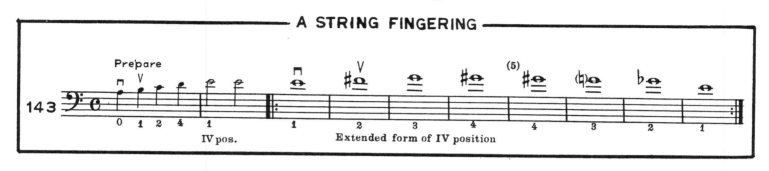

Before commencing, prepare for the EXTENDED FORM OF FOURTH POSITION by playing

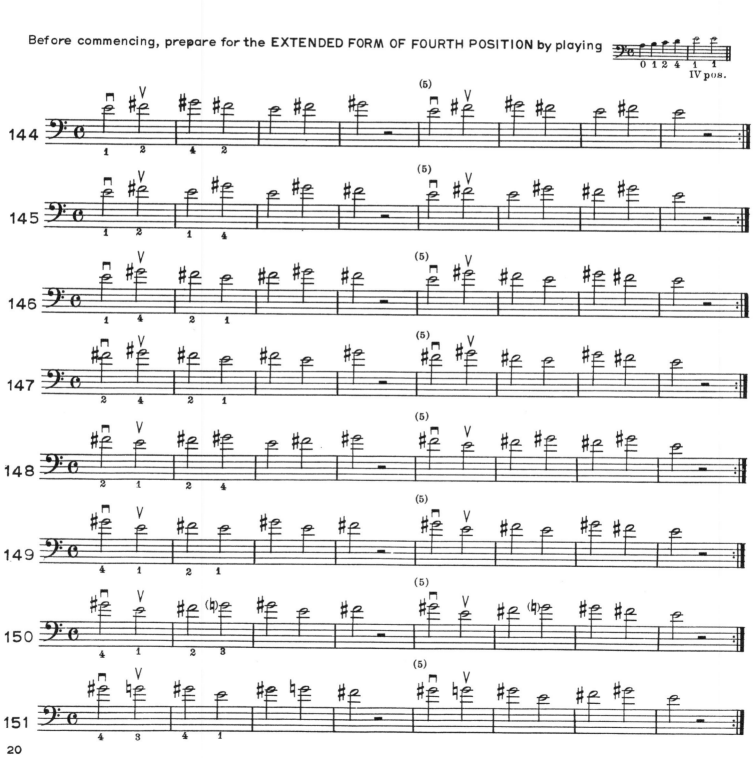

D String

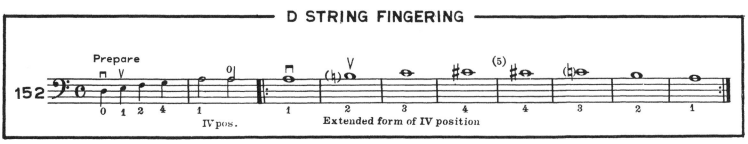

Before commencing, prepare for the EXTENDED FORM OF FOURTH POSITION by playing

G String

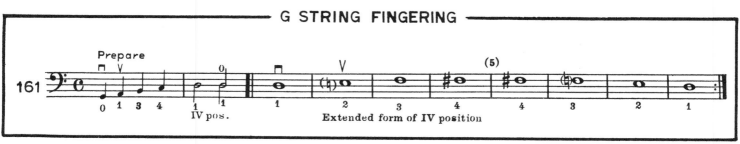

Before commencing, prepare for the EXTENDED FORM OF FOURTH POSITION by playing

C String

C STRING FINGERING

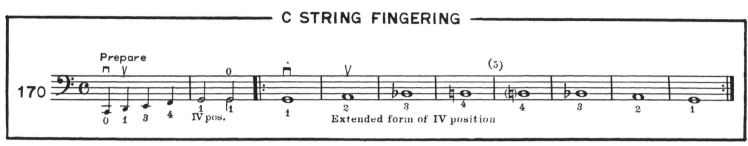

Before commencing, prepare for the EXTENDED FORM OF FOURTH POSITION by playing

Natural Harmonics

To produce a natural harmonic, merely touch the finger lightly against the string; do not press the finger down. ◊ = natural harmonic. Natural harmonics appear at various places on each string, but the most commonly used natural harmonic is the one which divides the string exactly in half from the nut to the bridge. This harmonic, which is played by the 3rd finger, extended from the fourth position, is known as the "half-string" harmonic.

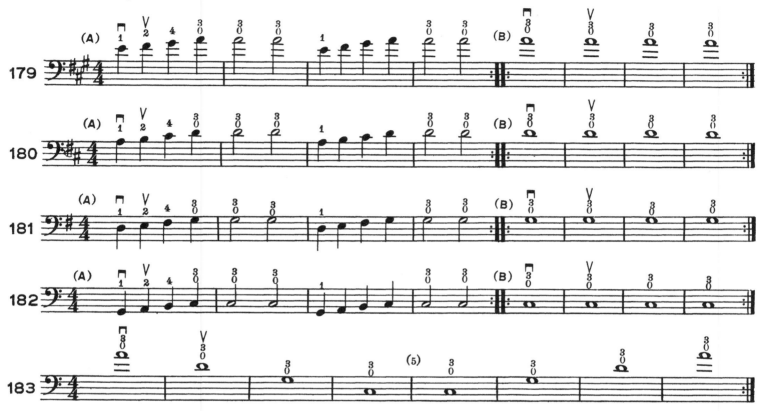

Shifting

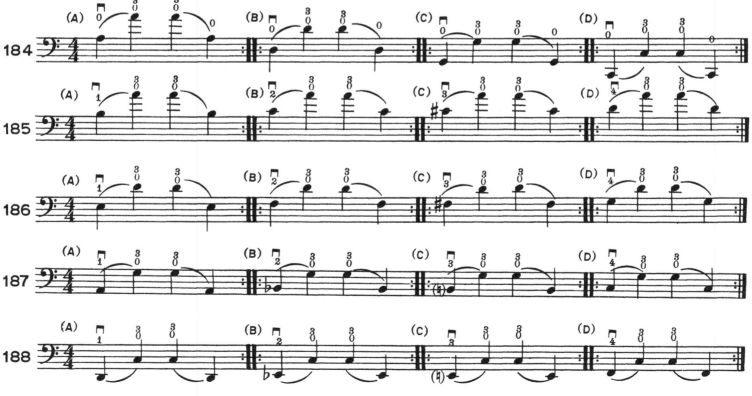

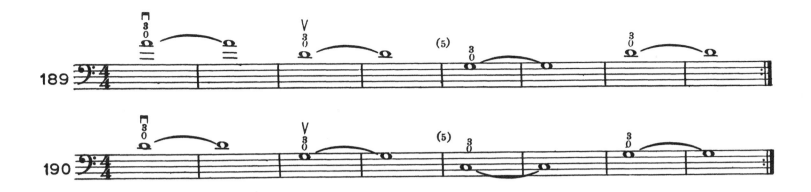

Open Strings and Harmonics

Fingered Tones and Harmonics

Also practice slurring each two tones.

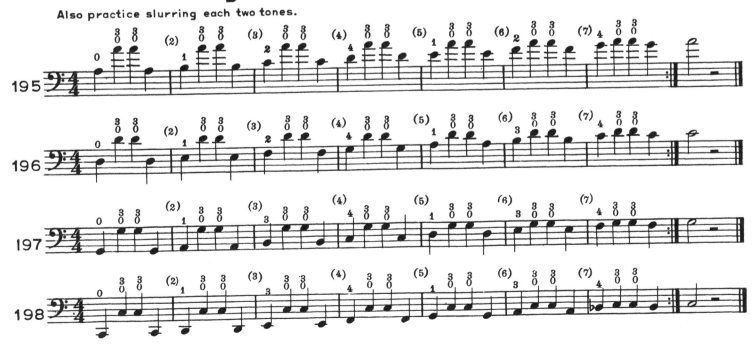

Half-String Harmonic Exercises

G STRING

C STRING

Technical Studies in Fourth Position
Natural Form

A STRING

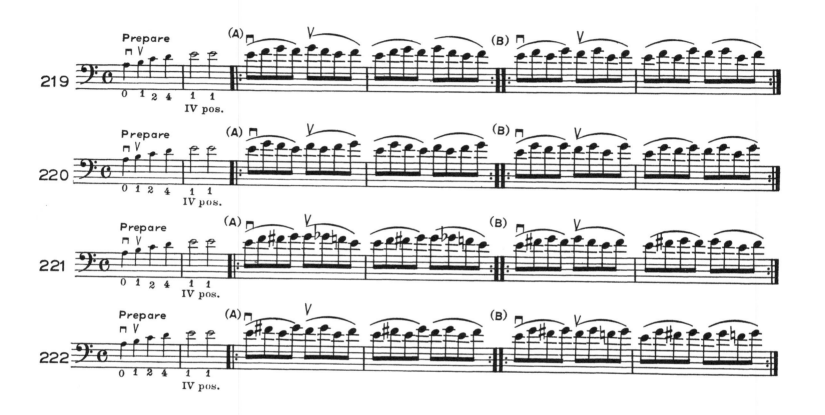

D STRING

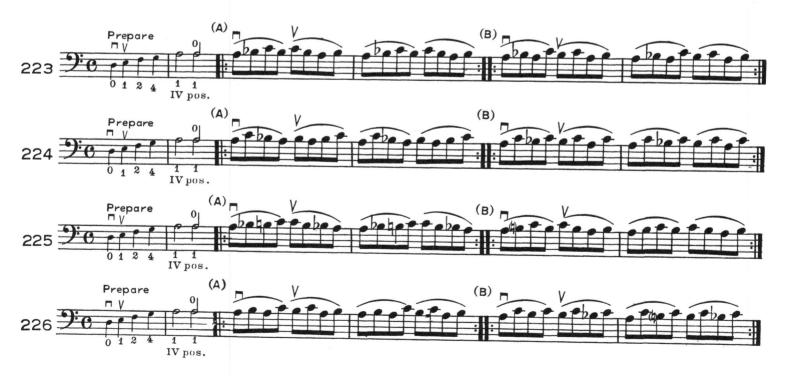

G STRING

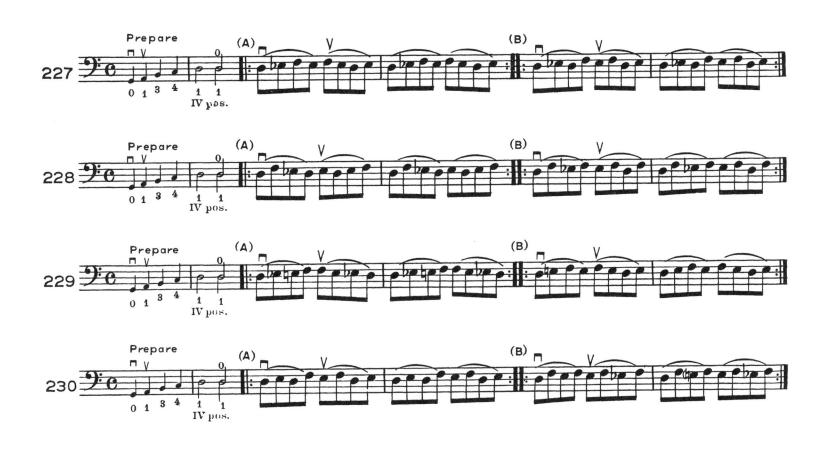

C STRING

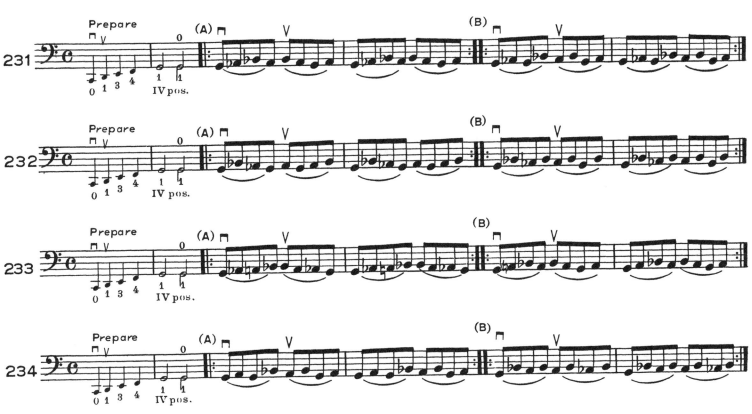

Lowered Form

A STRING

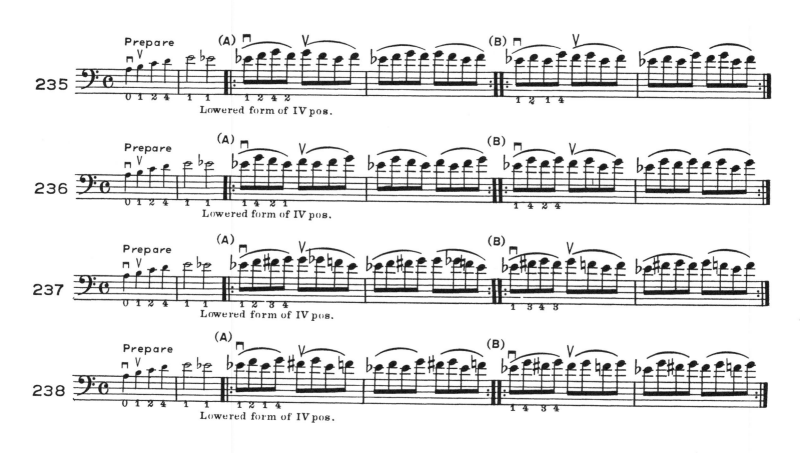

D STRING

G STRING

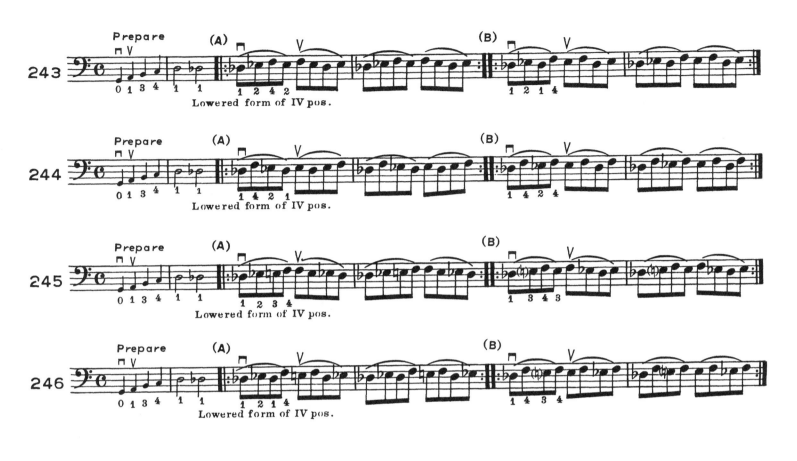

C STRING

Extended Form

A STRING

D STRING

G STRING

C STRING

Finger-Pattern Etudes in Fourth Position
Natural Form

1-2-4 Finger-pattern

Etude

WERNER

267

(Remain in Fourth Position.)

Etude

WERNER

268

(Remain in Fourth Position.)

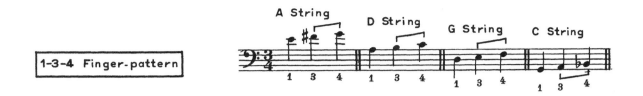

1-3-4 Finger-pattern

Etude

WERNER

269

(Remain in Fourth Position.)

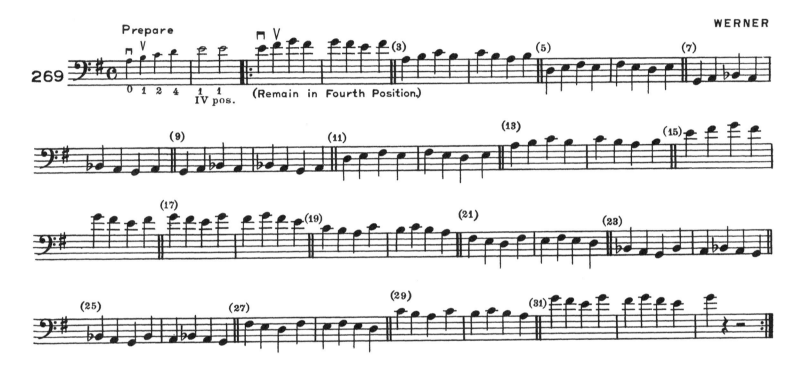

Etude

WERNER

270

(Remain in Fourth Position.)

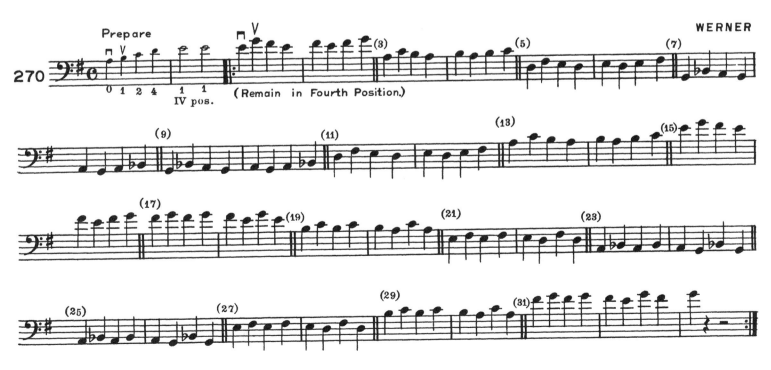

Lowered Form

1-2-4 Finger-pattern
(Lowered form)

Etude

WERNER

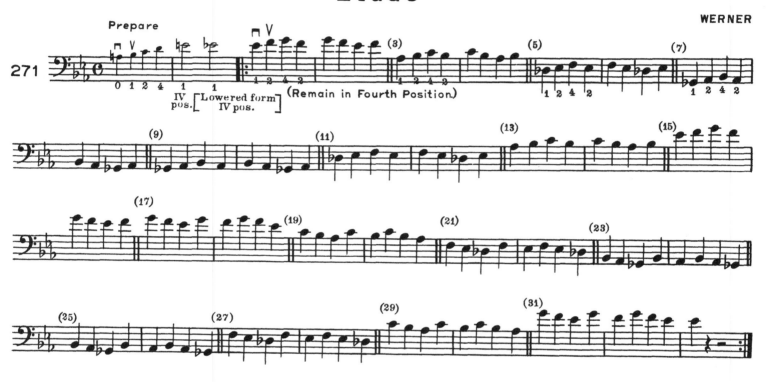

271

Etude

WERNER

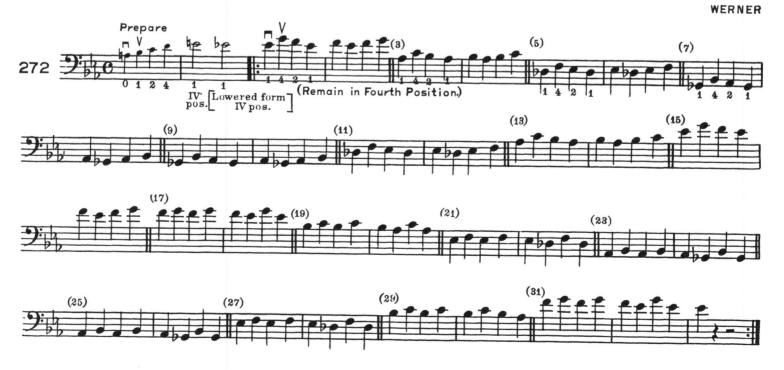

272

Extended Form

1-2-4 Finger-pattern (Extended form)

Etude

WERNER

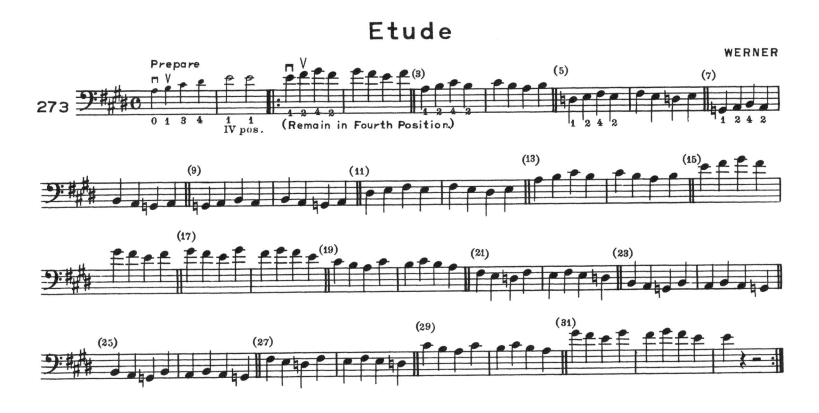

273

Etude

WERNER

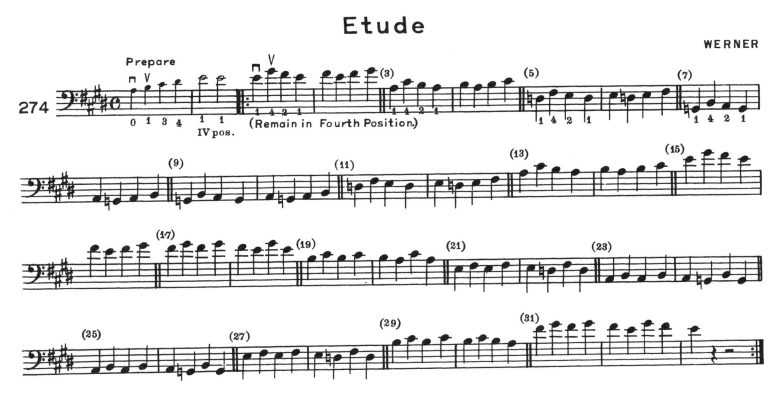

274

Etudes in the Fourth Position

Etude Melodique

WERNER

Etude Brillante

KUMMER

(Remain in Fourth Position.)

Etude Harmonique

WERNER

Etude Concertante

WERNER

Shifting Studies

In shifting from the first to higher position, remember NOT to take the finger up and put it down again; instead, SLIDE into the higher position.

Advanced Shifting from One Finger to Another

The student should remember to shift forward on the finger that was last down, and likewise, shift backward on the finger that was last down.

The student also should remember that the small note in the following exercises merely indicates the movement of the finger in shifting, and as the ability to shift from one note to another is perfected, the small note eventually should not be heard.

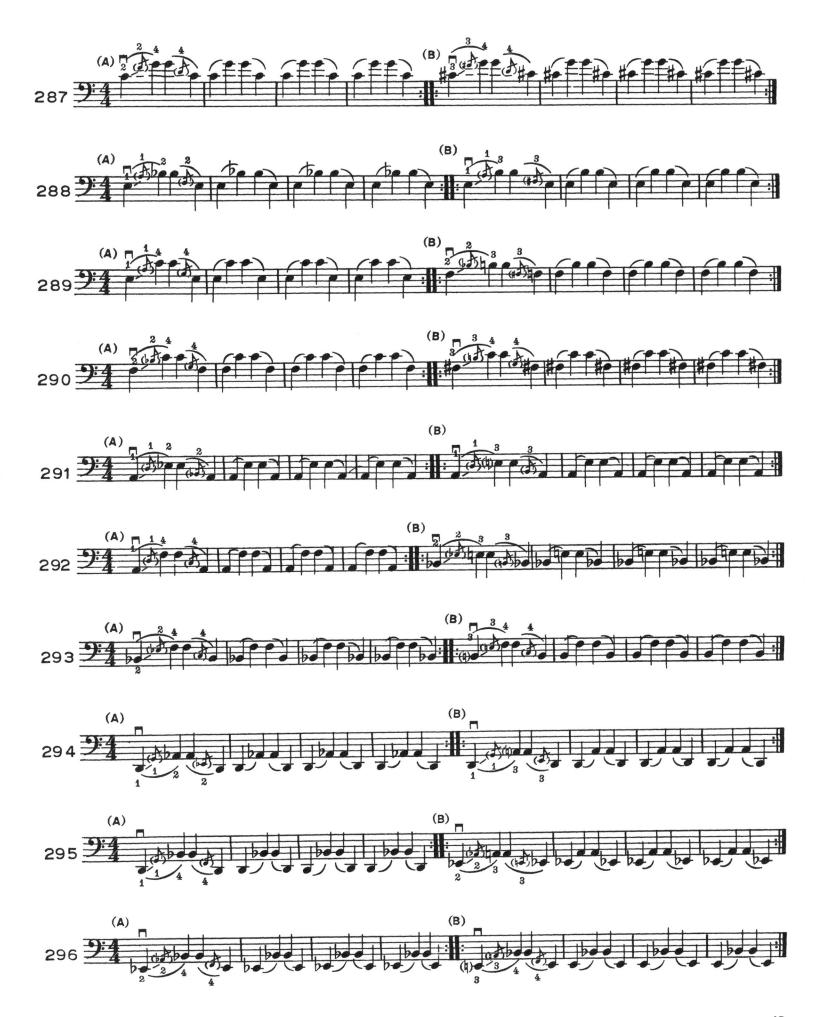

Advanced Shifting Studies

ADVANCED SHIFTING

SLURRED SHIFTING

STRING TO STRING SHIFTING

Scales in First and Fourth Positions

SCALE OF F MAJOR

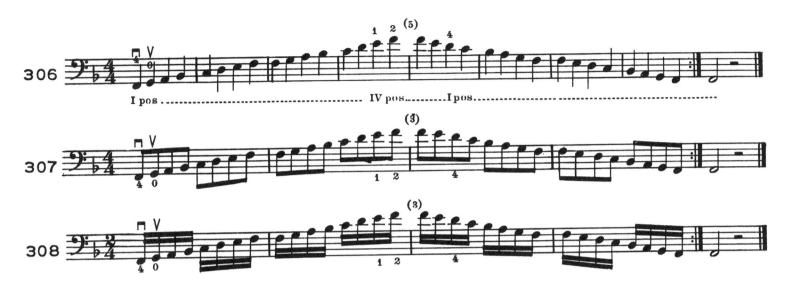

SCALE OF G MAJOR

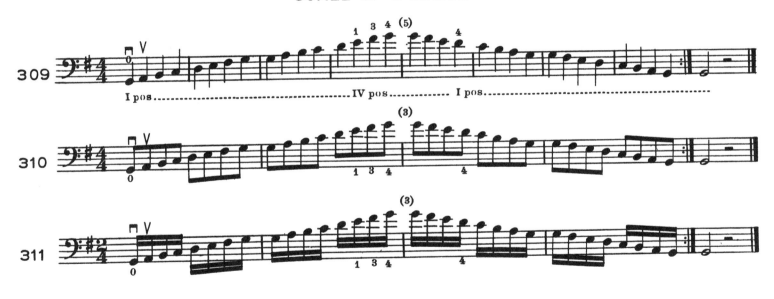

CHORDS IN FIRST AND FOURTH POSITIONS

Scale Exercises in First and Fourth Positions

A STRING

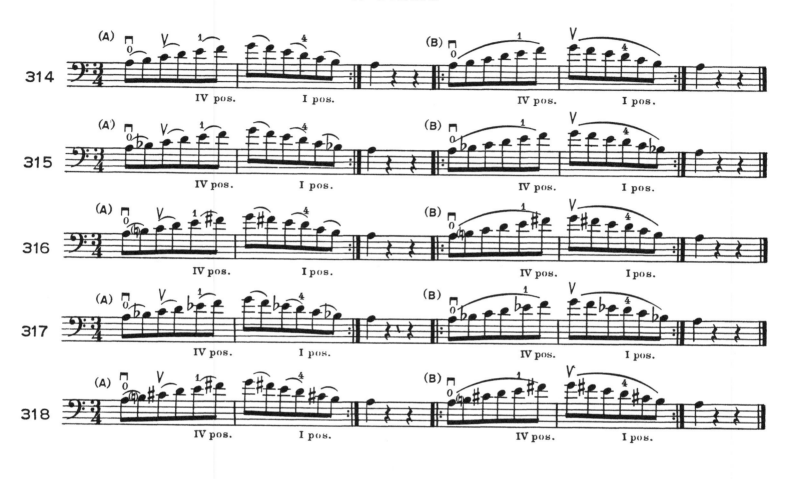

D STRING

G STRING

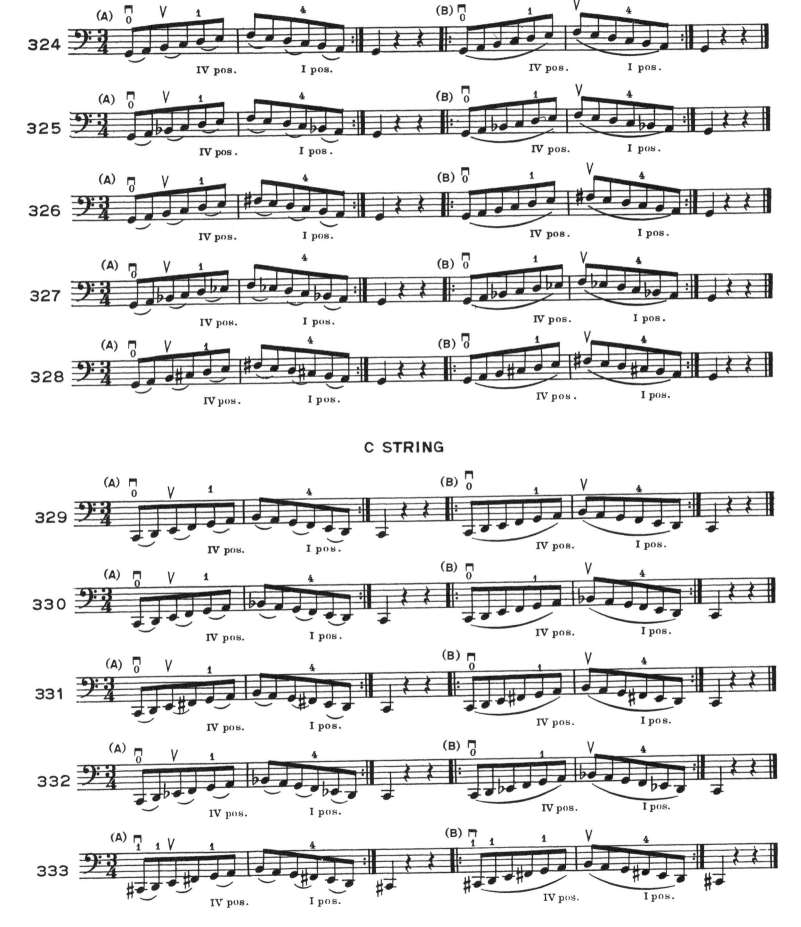

C STRING

Shifting Etude
(First and Fourth Positions)

Also practice slurring each two tones.

WERNER